FUN WITH CODES AND CIPHERS WORKBOOK

by Norma Gleason

DOVER PUBLICATIONS, INC. NEW YORK

With many, many thanks to my friend and fellow cryptology buff, Dr. Warren McCready of Canada, who not only proofread the text of this book but also proof-solved every one of the 68 ciphers in it in the interest of accuracy.

Published in Canada by General Publishing Company, Ltd., 30 Lesmill Road, Don Mills, Toronto, Ontario.
Published in the United Kingdom by Constable and Company, Ltd.

Fun with Codes and Ciphers Workbook is a new work, first published by Dover Publications, Inc., in 1987.

Manufactured in the United States of America
Dover Publications, Inc., 31 East 2nd Street, Mineola, N.Y. 11501

Library of Congress Cataloging-in-Publication Data

Gleason, Norma.
  Fun with codes and ciphers workbook.

  Bibliography: p.
  1. Ciphers.   I. Title.
Z104.G57   1987   652′.8   87-5228
ISBN 0-486-25405-4

Contents

Introduction

Sending and receiving secret messages is a fascinating hobby. In this workbook you will learn how to write (encipher) coded messages and how to read (decipher) them. (Traditionally, there is a technical difference between a *code* and a *cipher*. Often, however, the words are used interchangeably; we will do so in this book except in the chapter on "Codes" on page 36.)

Most of the ciphers in this book are of one of two major kinds, *transposition* and *substitution*. The transposition cipher uses the real letters of the message (*plaintext*) but mixes up the letters. The person who receives the message must put the letters back in the proper order.

A substitution cipher does not use the real letters of the message. Instead, other letters, numbers or symbols are substituted for them.

In all ciphers, a prearranged plan or method must be followed so that the person who receives the message can know how to set up the cipher so that it can be translated into plaintext (the original message). He either rearranges the letters of a transposition cipher, or makes the proper substitutions for the letters of a substitution cipher.

Each of these kinds of cipher—transposition and substitution—has many variations.

To make the best use of this book, you need a friend with whom you can exchange practice messages. He (or she) also needs a copy of this book, or you need to instruct him (or her) carefully in its methods and techniques.

This workbook is arranged so that you have plenty of work space. After each section of ciphers to solve, a page ruled in small squares is provided as a worksheet. Write neatly, keeping your rows and columns within the squares. If rows and columns are not uniform, you can get into trouble.

You will enjoy learning about, and practicing, the many kinds of secret writing explained in this book. Have fun!

Solutions to the ciphers are given at the back of the book, beginning on page 41.

● *Easy Transposition Ciphers*

Cipher 1

To get you started, here is an easy transposition cipher. Remember, in a transposition cipher all the real letters are there, but not in the normal order.

THGINOT ERUSAERT YRUB

This doesn't seem to make sense. But when you know the secret, it couldn't be easier to read. Just read the sentence backward, letter by letter! Write down what it says on the worksheet opposite.

Cipher 2

Here is another backward cipher.

SNRUTER YPPAH YNAM

Remember, all though this book, to write your answers (and solve the problems) on the worksheet so that you can compare them with the correct answers at the back of the book.

Cipher 3

The purpose of a secret message is, of course, privacy. The two ciphers above are too easy to read. What if we ran all the letters together without word divisions? Try this one.

NUFSISEGASSEMTERCESGNIDNES

That looks a bit more difficult. Write down the letters (starting from the end, of course, backward) and then separate them into words. What does the message say?

Cipher 4

Is there a still better way to write a backward cipher? Yes—you might throw interceptors off the track by using *false* word divisions:

T IROF KRO WOTE VAH U OYGN IHT EMO STNAW U

OYFI

As you can see, the false word divisions fool the eye. The reader thinks that each group of letters represents a word, and he cannot figure out how to interpret what he is looking at.

Cipher 5

Here is another one to do, with false word divisions.

H TEE TRIE H TW OH STONDLU OH SETIBTON

NAC OH WES OH T

Now, using the worksheet, try making up a few transposition ciphers of the kind explained here. Go back and check your work carefully. Did you make any mistakes? Mistakes are all too easy to make, but they will foul up your message so the person you want to read it may run into problems. Always check your work.

● *More Backward Ciphers*

Cipher 6

If we wish, we can write a backward cipher in a different way. We'll start out by writing the message backward but doing *each word* separately. Here is an example:

SRAIL DEEN DOOG SEIROMEM

If you try to read this backward from end to beginning, the words will not be in the right order. Instead, you read each word one at a time. What does the message say?

Cipher 7

A smart interceptor could easily read the cipher above. The idea of writing each word backward has merit, but we need to add a complication to disguise the method. So let us introduce false word divisions and a number key.

The message is first written backward a word at a time. Then false word divisions are made. Finally, a number key is given that tells your friend how many letters to read backward *at a time*.

6254 ERA WEBF OK CAL BSTAC

To read this, look at the numbers. The first number is 6. That tells you to take the first six letters ERAWEB and read them backward. Do the same with the next two letters. Read the message and check your answer on the answer page.

Cipher 8

427234 TEE MEMTH GIN OTTA DLOL LIM

Cipher 9

825747 RE THGUA LSID RAEH RE HTRUF NAH TGNIP EEW

Let's do one more with a number key.

Cipher 10

1–11–4–4–5–5–5 ADEHS AWET I HWW ORCNO OSS W OHSKC ALBNIAGA

Before leaving the backward cipher it would be well to introduce you to a useful way of grouping letters in cryptology, that is, in groups of five. The reason is that if you try to copy a long string of letters or numbers with no separation, it is easy to miss a letter. That, with some ciphers, could completely ruin your message. Instead of false word divisions in Cipher 10, the cipher could be written in groups of five, like this:

1–11–4–4–5–5–5 ADEHS AWETI HWWOR CNOOS SWOHS KCALB NIAGA

If the message does not have five letters remaining at the end, just use one, two, three or four letters as needed. You will be working with five-letter groups later in this workbook.

● *The Null Cipher*

The null cipher is neither a transposition cipher nor a substitution cipher. It is included with the transpositions only because it resembles that type of cryptogram more than it does substitution, since all the real letters of the message are there. In the null cipher, meaningless letters that are not part of the message are thrown in to cause confusion. Suppose we take the name JOE and write it like this: B J P O S E. If you read every other letter, JOE is spelled out. The B, P and S are nulls—letters that mean nothing.

In order to make use of the null cipher, you must arrange with your friend beforehand that every other letter will be read. Or every third letter. Or the last letter in each group—whatever arrangement you like. The order of the letters in the message is never changed in a null cipher, except that the message as a whole is sometimes read backward.

Try your hand at these nulls.

Cipher 11

Read the third letter of each "word."

BXTYS SSHBW POILL WQSDA TYIYH PKSRE NMAAO

OPNIK QPUML ERLET MNLJI POCMN YUIER NNPOL

SGHPW GXENT LLRKI

Only the third letter of each word counts. All the other letters are nulls. Notice that real words were not used in the above cipher, just groups of random letters except for the third letter.

Cipher 12

Shirley
Edith
Nancy
Dave
Hal
Ernie
Lionel
Paul

Writing the null cipher in the form of a list makes it appear quite innocent. But if you read the first letter of each word in order, downward, a message is revealed. What is the message?

Cipher 13

Austin, Texas
Trenton, New Jersey
Honolulu, Hawaii
Madison, Wisconsin
Asheville, North Carolina
Cheyenne, Wyoming
Baltimore, Maryland
Joplin, Missouri

Or you can list cities—this would appear equally innocent. If you read the third letter of each city name, reading down, what message is revealed?

Make up a null or two of your own on the worksheet. Then go on to a few more nulls on the next page.

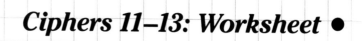

● *More Null Ciphers*

Cipher 14

Here is another list-type null. This time we've listed some German words. You don't need to know a foreign language to make up this kind of null. Just borrow a foreign-language dictionary.

WASSER

ONKEL

RADIO

RAUM

OBST

MARMELADE

ORANGE

TOMATE

MILCH

POST

OKTOBER

WEG

TORTE

EULE

NACHBAR

ANDRANG

LANDKARTE

PULT

TULPE

ERSATZ

ENERGIE

MORGEN

See if you can figure out what this null cipher says—in English, of course. Try everything.

Cipher 15

Another way to write a null cipher is to send a message in which only certain words count, the others being null words (rather than null letters). Suppose that jewel thieves are planning a robbery. The following code message is sent:

HAVE GALLERY VAN AT SITE TONIGHT STOP

OPENING DISPLAY PICASSO PAINTINGS STOP

DUE TIME LIMITATIONS FAST UNLOADING

NECESSARY STOP TAKE PAINTINGS LOBBY

OFF MAIN GALLERY STOP PUBLICITY ARRANGED

The thieves have agreed on a keyword, BUMPY, to send the message. They first wrote out the real message. Then they added other words—null words—to confuse. To ferret out the real message, go through the telegram carefully, crossing out all words that contain any of the five letters in BUMPY. What words are left?

● *Columnar Transpositions*

Now we go on to a more difficult cipher.

You already know what a transposition cipher is—one that transposes, or changes the position of, the real letters of a message. So what is a "columnar" transposition? It's one that changes the position of *columns*.

First, be sure you know the difference between a row and a column.

The letters ABC are in a row. The letters A are in a
column.   B
          C

In a columnar transposition you write the message out in short *rows*. You then switch around the *columns*.

As an example, we'll write the message TAKE GOOD CARE:

```
1 2 3

T A K      Notice how the words are written in the
           block at left. Four rows of letters and three
E G O      columns of letters. This is the first step in
           constructing this kind of cipher.
O D C

A R E
```

Next we switch the columns around; let's decide on a 2–1–3 order. That is, the column numbered 2 above becomes the first column and so on:

```
2 1 3

A T K      The same letters appear in each row and
           each column, but the three columns have
G E O      been rearranged. Rearranging the columns
           is the second step.
D O C

R A E
```

The third and last step is to "take off" (copy) the letters by *column*: AGDR TEOA KOCE, or, in groups of five letters each, AGDRT EOAKO CE.

This makes a good cipher—but how will your friend know how to read it?

You and your friend agree on three things at the start. One, you will use the columnar-transposition method for your cipher messages. Two, all messages will be written in three columns and as many rows as needed. If a message does not fill out a row completely at the end, you add one or two X's as needed to fill it out. Three, the deciphering arrangement will always be 2–1–3. Then your friend will know how to lay out the cipher for translating into plaintext.

To learn the procedure, use the worksheet to work out our example. Do not look at the instructions unless you get stuck. Write TAKE GOOD CARE at the top of the worksheet. Then write that message in a block, three letters at a time in *rows*. Rearrange the columns. Last of all, take off the cipher in groups of five letters.

Next, take the cipher you just wrote out (the cipher sentence in five-letter groups) and reverse the steps. In other words, decipher the message. Do all this on your worksheet. If necessary, read the instructions again. Then try deciphering this one:

Cipher 16

HTOEG STIOS RS

● *More Columnar Transpositions*

Solve the following ciphers using the same technique.

Cipher 17

TSEGT BLFPH TGESR RINCL OURAD SAAGA IASSE
EEAS

Remember to count the letters and divide by three so you know how long to make the columns.

Cipher 18

SLSUE AESST NSAHA IICVH HPOTI SRGME ARTTL
TEHGT IT

Cipher 19

HOIHR RKIEI ARTFL ARDNH TWHOE ONUYI SSATF K

Do you understand the way columnar transpositions work? Then go on to a four-column cipher. If you aren't yet sure how to do these, practice on the worksheet, following the examples given at the top of this page. For a four column, the method is the same, but you count the words and divide by four instead of three to find the length of the columns. Try this four-column:

Cipher 20

YPLTN ONNSN BENEO OFTSO TTIBL NPUOH AWVIM
WOTEE OEUDA EZA

(48 letters, divided by 4 = 12, length of columns—assume a 4–2–3–1 arrangement.)

Cipher 21

Here is another four-column. This time, we had to add X's to fill out the bottom row of letters. The column arrangement is not 4–2–3–1. Try to find the right rearrangement by looking for words in the *rows*. Tip: The word CAN appears.

MGDNB WXUNR AYKDH IICLC RMBSF AAX

Cipher 22

Using the worksheet, construct a four-column cipher, adding X's where needed. Use the 4–2–3–1 rearrangement to take off the final sentence cipher. Be careful. Then check your work in the answer section to see if you did it correctly. Use this message:

DO NOT ASK THE WAY OF A BLIND MAN

If you like, you can develop the columnar transposition further. Use the worksheet or extra paper to make up five-column and six-column transpositions. Remember to add the X's at the end if needed.

Are you wondering why you always need to add X's to fill out the bottom row? After you have constructed the four-column "blind man" cipher *with* X's, try constructing it *without* the X's. Then try to *decipher* the final sentence cipher. Impossible, because the columns are not of equal length. You will not be able to recover the correct message—it will be garbled.

● Route Transpositions

Let us move on now to a different kind of transposition cipher, the *route transposition*. A route is a path, a road, a direction. In this cipher, you write your message in a block, following a certain path or route, then take it off in a cipher sentence.

Let's say we want to use the route transposition method to send the message GOOD LUCK. We will write it in the four ways below, following, as you can see, different paths or routes:

Route 1		Route 2	
D	K	G	O
O	C	D	O
O	U	L	U
G	L	K	C

Route 3		Route 4	
D	L	G	O
O	U	K	O
O	C	C	D
G	K	U	L

Route 1 is written upward by columns.

Route 2 is written in rows alternating from forward to backward.

Route 3 is written in columns alternating from upward to downward.

Route 4 is written in a clockwise spiral, starting at top left.

Follow these paths, spelling out GOOD LUCK, so you see how it is done.

Cipher 23

To get the hang of it, write HAPPY TIMES in the same four ways. Then check your layouts in the answer section to see if you did them correctly. With this cipher, you will have five letters per column instead of four.

Cipher 24

HISAN AFBHN IAETO FOTRN ALTEE

Solve this cipher by writing it in rows, five letters per row. Read the message by *columns*, first down, then up.

Cipher 25

TBOOU HLWST EETDW ROHNA ENAER ISTBD

Write out the cipher the same way, in a block, in rows of five letters at a time. Read the same way as the one you just did, in alternating columns.

Cipher 26

TILIS WHMKR TOEPF UOCBE ROLEE EOSEH SKMGA
TTOGN VNWTE IEIAY TTIT

If you were not told in advance how to write out and then read this cipher, how would you go about it? It's easy, as long as you know that it is a route transposition. Count the letters. This cipher has 54 letters in it. Now, what two numbers multiplied together equal 54? You need to know this in order to know how many letters go in each row and column. $6 \times 9 = 54$. Or 9×6. It could be 2×27 or 27×2, but in this kind of cipher such a variation is seldom used.

Try writing the cipher out, six letters at a time per row. Figure out how to read it. The route, or path, used to write the original message in a block is not always the same as the path used to read it. That is, one route may be used for writing the message, another path for taking off the cipher.

What does the cipher say?

● *Easy Substitution Ciphers*

The time has come for you to change your way of thinking about ciphers. Those you have studied so far (backward ciphers, nulls, columnar transpositions and route transpositions) are *transposition ciphers*—ciphers in which the real letters of a message are present but arranged differently.

Let's look at ciphers that do not contain the real letters of a message. In a *substitution cipher*, false letters or numbers or symbols are substituted for the real letters. For example, a plaintext R may be a cipher B, or an asterisk (*), or a 6.

The easiest kind of substitution cipher is the Caesar cipher, named after Julius Caesar, who used it to send secret messages when at war. Examine this pair of alphabets:

Note that each substitute letter is the letter that follows the real letter in the regular alphabet—A becomes B and B becomes C and so on.

Example: S E P T E M B E R in cipher, using the alphabets below, becomes:

T F Q U F N C F S

As in transposition ciphers, the letters of the original message are called *plaintext*; the substitute letters are called *ciphertext*.

Try solving this easy Caesar. Use the pair of alphabets below. Remember, you have to go *back* one letter in deciphering because the cipher was written ahead one letter.

Real letters: A B C D E F G H I J K L M N O P Q R S T U V W X Y Z

Substitutes: B C D E F G H I J K L M N O P Q R S T U V W X Y Z A

Cipher 27

EFBE NFO UFMM OP UBMFT

Cipher 28

Do this one the same way:

POF PME GSJFOE JT CFUUFS UIBO UXP OFX POFT

Now for some practice work. On the worksheet, set up four alphabets, the first beginning with A, the second with B, the third with C and the fourth with D. Be sure to finish off each row—Z is followed by A. And be very sure to line up the alphabets exactly.

Make ciphers from the following short texts. Use the A alphabet for the plaintext. For each cipher, use the designated alphabet.

Cipher 29

Use the B cipher alphabet: THE STATUE OF LIBERTY

Cipher 30

Use the C cipher alphabet: THE PEANUT IS A FRUIT, NOT A NUT

Cipher 31

Use the D cipher alphabet: A PRUNE IS A PLUM THAT HAS SEEN BETTER DAYS

Check your work in the answer section. Did you make any mistakes?

● *More Substitution Ciphers*

The Caesar ciphers were constructed with word lengths untouched. But as you know, it is better not to give away the lengths of words. The Caesar ciphers on this page will be presented in five-letter groups. It's up to you to sort out the words. Also you will decide for yourself how many letters backward to go for deciphering. You do this by trial and error. If the first few letters of a decoding don't make sense, you are using the wrong cipher alphabet.

The following alphabet layout should be helpful. Lay a ruler under the alphabet that proves to be correct for each problem.

Work out the ciphers on this page.

Plain:	A B C D E F G H I J K L M N O P Q R S T U V W X Y Z
Cipher:	B C D E F G H I J K L M N O P Q R S T U V W X Y Z A
	C D E F G H I J K L M N O P Q R S T U V W X Y Z A B
	D E F G H I J K L M N O P Q R S T U V W X Y Z A B C
	E F G H I J K L M N O P Q R S T U V W X Y Z A B C D
	F G H I J K L M N O P Q R S T U V W X Y Z A B C D E

Cipher 32

JGBOU TBSFT PCVTZ IPXDP NFUIF ZIBWF UJNFU

PBUUF OEBMM UIFQJ DOJDT

Cipher 33

WKHZL QGVKL HOGZL SHUZD VLQYH QWHGV

RSROL FHZRX OGKDY HDSOD FHWRS XWSDU

NLQJW LFNHW V

Cipher 34

NJFYR DUJFX BNYMM TSJDN AJITS JNYFQ QRDQN

KJNYR FPJXY MJUJF XYFXY JKZSS DGZYN YPJJU

XYMJR TSYMJ PSNKJ

Cipher 35

ELSWT MXEPM WETPE GIALI VITIS TPIAL SEVIV

YRHSA RAMRH YT

Cipher 36

VCDNG VGPPK UKUVJ GWPQH HKEKC NURQT

VQHEJ KPC

Before we leave the Caesar cipher, look again at the set of alphabets above. We have been using the normal A–Z alphabet for plaintext all along, and the others for ciphertext. Using the B cipher alphabet, the word SUCCESS becomes TVDDFTT.

But we may turn things around, and use any of the cipher alphabets for our plaintext, and the normal alphabet for our cipher. If we use the B alphabet for plaintext and the top or normal alphabet for cipher, we will get a different cipher word for SUCCESS: RTBBDRR instead of TVDDFTT.

Here is an example, using the B alphabet as plaintext:

Cipher 37

HAL

Short and sweet, but there's a story here. Hal was the name of a highly computerized robot in a television story. His name was not chosen by accident. To find out what it stands for, go *forward* one letter instead of back as you have been doing.

Use the worksheet to lay out new alphabets (you are not limited to those we have used; try a cipher alphabet beginning with L, if you like.) Construct short ciphers of your own, for practice.

● *More Easy Substitution Ciphers*

Plain:	A B C D E F G H I J K L M N O P Q R S T U V W X Y Z
Cipher:	Z Y X W V U T S R Q P O N M L K J I H G F E D C B A

Let us move on now to other simple methods for putting together a substitution cipher. Examine the alphabet pair above:

The cipher alphabet is written backward, while the plaintext alphabet remains as before.

Note that this is not the same as a Caesar starting with Z. If it were a Caesar, the letter after Z would be A and the normal alphabet would follow.

Using the above alphabets, plain A becomes cipher Z, plain B becomes cipher Y and so on. A peculiarity of this system is that the alphabets are reciprocal: if plain A = cipher Z, then plain Z = cipher A. This is not so with most alphabet pairs.

Using the alphabets above, solve these two ciphers:

Cipher 38

GSV WZXSHSFMW RH Z WLT GSZG RH LMOB SZOU

Z WLT SRTS YFG Z WLT ZMW Z SZOU OLMT

Cipher 39

GSVNL HGDZH GVWLU ZOOWZ BHRHG SVWZB

DSVMD VSZEV MLGOZ FTSVW

To become familiar with this type of substitution, make up a cipher or two of your own on the worksheet, using the reverse alphabet for the cipher.

Another way to set up a cipher alphabet is with a keyword. Let's use the word PRIVATE as a keyword:

Two things must be pointed out about keyboard cipher alphabets. First, all letters contained in the keyword (in this case, PRIVATE) are omitted from the rest of the alphabet. Another point to note is that PRIVATE does not *begin* the cipher alphabet.

Plain:	A B C D E F G H I J K L M N O P Q R S T U V W X Y Z
Cipher:	N O Q S U W X Y Z P R I V A T E B C D F G H J K L M

Cipher 40

To find out why you would not begin the cipher alphabet with the keyword, set up an alphabet pair on your worksheet. Use the normal plaintext alphabet, but start the ciphertext with the keyword, PRIVATE. Then continue with the normal alphabet, omitting the letters in PRIVATE. What happens? Check your answer in the answer section.

Using the keyword alphabet, decipher the next two cryptograms (a *cryptogram* is a message in cipher that is used for secret communication):

Cipher 41

ZW LTG YNHU NA ZFQY FT JCZFU FYU OUDF FYZAX

FT GDU ZD N DQCNFQY ENS

Cipher 42

QTADQZUAQU ZD FYU HTZQU FYNF FUIID LTG ATF

FT ST DTVUFYZAX NWFUC LTG YNHU STAU ZF

20

● *Random Substitution Ciphers*

Would you like to learn how to solve the cryptograms in newspapers and magazines? They are a different kind of animal. They are substitution ciphers, but the letters in the cipher alphabet are mixed up in no particular order. This makes the cipher much more difficult to solve unless you have a copy of the mixed cipher alphabet on hand.

Let Little Orphan Annie introduce you to this kind of cryptogram. In the old days of radio, the Orphan Annie program was broadcast weekly. At the end of each broadcast a cipher message was read over the air, consisting of numbers. The youngsters copied down the numbers and then turned to their "Orphan Annie Secret Decoder" to translate the message. The decoder, which kids got by sending in box tops, contained the normal alphabet and a mixed-up, or random, cipher alphabet.

Cipher 43

Here is a real Orphan Annie message from the year 1938:

```
17 24 15 03 24 11 09    08 03 23 23 25 23

20 02 03 06 11 03 08    21 24 21 21 01

06 24 19 12 02 17 18 08
```

Suppose you were a youngster way back then, listening to the Little Orphan Annie program, but did not have a decoder. Could you solve the cipher anyway? You probably could if you were a regular listener. You could guess at some of the words and see if those letters worked out in other words. Usually the message was short and told what the next episode was about. The names of characters nearly always appeared in the message. The main characters were Annie, her dog Sandy and Daddy Warbucks. Others included Captain Steele.

Look at the cipher word 21 24 21 21 01. It is what

cryptologists (a *cryptologist* is one who specializes in the study of ciphers) call a *pattern word*, because it has repeated letters. What character listed above has a name that fits the pattern? ANNIE? No:

$$\frac{21\ \ 24\ \ 21\ \ 21\ \ 01}{A\ \ \ \ N\ \ \ N\ \ \ I\ \ \ E}$$

The first, third and fourth numbers are the same, so the first, third and fourth letters in the name must also be the same. Look again at the names of some of the characters. What name does fit?

Copy the number cipher on your worksheet. Leave room under each line to write the letters. Fill in the right name for 21 24 21 21 01. Wherever the number 21 appears in the cipher, put the correct letter beneath it. Do the same with the other numbers that you have identified. You should then be able to figure out the last word in the cipher. See if you can finish solving this cryptogram by guessing at the remaining cipher words.

Cipher 44

Solve this by finding where each of the following pattern words fits and filling in those letters throughout the cipher: SCHOOL, LITTLE, WHERE, SIS, LEARNED. Copy the cipher on your worksheet, leaving room between lines. And keep track of the letters you identify. Don't give the same cipher letter more than one identity.

SPGGSX APSSPX, MRJX NLRJ BZMRRS,

AMXLX MX SXHLVXF GMX QRSFXV LDSX,

BHPF, "PN P XHG DT GMPB ZHWX,

BPB ARV'G MHEX H BGRJHZM HZMX."

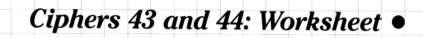

● *More About Random Substitutions*

Some pattern words that often appear in cryptograms are TOO, ALL, EVER, THAT, WERE, WHERE, EVERY, LITTLE and BETTER. In trying to solve newspaper or magazine cryptograms, look for pattern words that might be these.

Also look for a one-letter word. It is usually A, sometimes I, once in a great while some other letter (as in Vitamin D).

A three-letter word, especially if it begins the cipher, may be THE. That word appears in English writings over and over. Pick up a book or magazine, turn to any page, and count how many times you see THE in a paragraph.

If you think a three-letter word might be THE, examine the cipher to see if the cipher letters for T and E are generously sprinkled throughout. They should be of high frequency. Also, the letter E often ends words, so check to see if this is the case. (Four words in the last sentence end with E, not counting the capital E.) If so, you are probably right about the three-letter cipher word being THE.

Letters that ordinarily are of high frequency, besides E, are (in order of decreasing frequency) TAOINSHR.

Try solving this random-substitution cipher. Copy it carefully on your worksheet.

Cipher 45

VR JDM YVZLJ BXJF ZBPM MSMZ DMOH, CFZM

JDBR RVRMJK KMBZL BUF, JDM GVRRMZ

BSMZBUMH B LNMMH FY LMSMR BRH B DBOY

CVOML NMZ DFXZ

Tips: First find the one-letter word. Try A for that letter throughout the cipher. Next try to identify the word THE. You should then be able to guess the ninth word. (It is not a pattern word, is it?) Then guess at other words. The cipher is about the early days of the automobile.

Cipher 46

EFM KTCL VEREM ZT EFZV DKYTEQL AFMQM

IZRBKTIV DRT SM HKYTI ZV *RQPRTVRV. EKYQZVEV

RQM RCCKAMI EK IZX HKQ EFMB

There are no one-letter words in this cipher. But look at the first word. Does it meet the test for THE? If it does, fill in all the T's, H's and E's. Then look for a pattern word with H and E in it. (It is in the short list given above.) What is the last cipher word? The starred word is the name of a state. What state name fits that pattern?

Cipher 47

YBC WCYYCA C VP YBC XCLVZZVZL KR CYCAZVYU

YBC CZN KR YVHC FZN PEFTC YBC XCLVZZVZL KR

CMCAU CZN YBC CZN KR CMCAU EWFTC

Tips: The word THE is here several times. The one-letter word, strangely enough, is neither A nor I (remember Vitamin D—but it's not a D, either!). Look for a pattern word. Also, the word BEGINNING appears twice.

You can see that solving cryptograms without knowing the cipher alphabet is light-years away from solving one when you have the solving key at hand. Learning to solve newspaper and magazine cryptograms is like learning to ride a bicycle. It took practice before you became skilled, but one day you said, "Look, Ma, no hands!" The more cryptograms you try to solve, the more you will learn. In time you can do them with ease.

● *Easy Telephone Ciphers*

A = 21	G = 41	M = 61	T = 81
B = 22	H = 42	N = 62	U = 82
C = 23	I = 43	O = 63	V = 83
D = 31	J = 51	P/Q = 71	W = 91
E = 32	K = 52	R = 72	X = 92
F = 33	L = 53	S = 73	Y/Z = 93

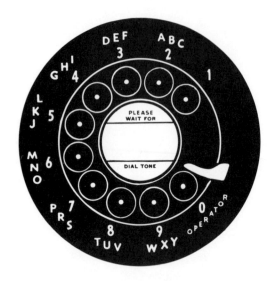

Your home telephone provides an easy way for you and a friend to exchange secret messages. The telephone dial can be used as a coding device. Look at the list above, starting with A = 21. You use the number 21 for A, 22 for B and so on.

But you don't want to leave this list around where someone could find it and decipher your secret messages. You do not need this list at all! The same information can be found right on your telephone dial, always ready when you want to use it.

Notice that you need two numbers to represent each letter of the alphabet. Let's see how we got the number 21 for A. First, notice on the dial that the letters above the number 2 are ABC. Also notice that A is the first of the three letters, B the second and C the third. The number 2 identifies the ABC grouping, and the number 1 identifies the first letter of that grouping—21.

On your worksheet, write down the cipher numbers for the word HELP. Do not look at the list, but rather use the telephone dial. Then check the list to make sure you did it correctly and understand the method.

Then go ahead and solve these telephone ciphers:

Cipher 48

81 42 32   23 72 63 91   43 73   21

22 43 72 31   81 42 21 81   62 32 83 32 72

23 63 61 71 53 21 43 62 73

91 43 81 42 63 82 81   23 21 91 73

Cipher 49

53 32 81 81 43 62 41   81 42 32   23 21 81

63 82 81   63 33   81 42 32   22 21 41

43 73   61 82 23 42

32 21 73 43 32 72   81 63   31 63

81 42 21 62   71 82 81 81 43 62 41   43 81

22 21 23 52

Cipher 50

21   23 63 61 71 82 81 32 72   43 73

21 53 61 63 73 81   42 82 61 21 62

32 92 23 32 71 81   43 81

62 32 83 32 72   22 53 21 61 32 73

43 81 73   61 43 73 81 21 52 32 73

63 62   63 81 42 32 72

23 63 61 71 82 81 32 72 73

Use the extra space on your worksheet to write out some telephone ciphers of your own. Have a friend check your ciphers to see if you made any errors.

● *More Telephone Ciphers*

You may have noticed on page 26 that pattern words show up in number ciphers just as in letter ciphers when word lengths are kept. The word A is repeated as 21 and THAT as 81 42 21 81. That makes the cipher easier for unwanted solvers to crack.

Try this telephone cipher with word lengths hidden:

Cipher 51

43 81 43	73 42 21	72 31 33	63 72 21
62 32 61	71 81 93	73 21 23	52 81 63
73 81 21	62 31 82	71 72 43	41 42 81

Cipher 52

This time we'll toss in some null letters. All of the letters in this cipher are nulls. Only the numbers are to be considered.

21P53	53BXW	23EES	5332S	21P72
33XBS	63O72	72B21	43EES	3181B
63B62	A43AP	A4142	S81MP	

Suppose someone good at ciphers got hold of your telephone cipher messages. Studying either of the ciphers above, he might notice something odd. Although the first number in each pair goes from 1 through 9, the second number never goes beyond 3. Pondering this, he might recognize the telephone cipher. We can prevent this by using null numbers instead of null letters. For nulls we can use any pair of numbers ending in 4, 5, 6, 7, 8 or 9.

In the following cipher, ignore the first number of each pair for the time being, but cross out all pairs that end in 4, 5, 6, 7, 8 or 9. Then solve the cipher that is left.

Cipher 53

63 48 62	79 79 32	35 71 32	72 48 26
73 63 62	44 54 73	79 73 81	29 35 82
61 22 26	53 55 19	43 62 41	22 26 53
55 19 63	27 19 23	52 43 73	21 48 62
63 81 42	48 26 32	72 79 55	73 73 81
32 19 18	71 71 43	62 41 49	79 73 81
63 62 65	32		

An alternative telephone cipher: Instead of using two numbers like 63 or 48 to identify a single letter, you use one number with a mark above it. A mark slanting to the left represents the first of the three letters on the dial grouping. A mark that goes straight up stands for the second letter, and if the mark slants to the right it stands for the third letter. Example:

$$A = \overset{\backslash}{2} \qquad B = \overset{|}{2} \qquad C = \overset{/}{2}$$

Solve the following cipher constructed in that manner.

Cipher 54

/||/\	||/\\|	|\\|/\	\\||\\
6 6 3 2 2	6 6 6 8 3	9 7 3 2 8	8 4 3 9 2
\/|\ /	\\/|/	\\||/\	/|//
8 2 4 3 6	4 8 6 2 4	8 3 4 4 6	7 3 5 3

● *Sir Francis Bacon's Cipher*

This cipher is named after its inventor, Sir Francis Bacon. It has an advantage and a disadvantage. The advantage: You may use this cipher in ways that would not be possible with other ciphers (more on this later). The disadvantage: It takes five cipher letters or symbols to represent one plaintext letter. A message of 50 letters, then, would become a cipher message of 250 letters!

Let's see how it works.

A = aaaaa	N = abbaa
B = aaaab	O = abbab
C = aaaba	P = abbba
D = aaabb	Q = abbbb
E = aabaa	R = baaaa
F = aabab	S = baaab
G = aabba	T = baaba
H = aabbb	U/V = baabb
I/J = abaaa	W = babaa
K = abaab	X = babab
L = ababa	Y = babba
M = ababb	Z = babbb

The chart above is used for creating the cipher message. You and your friend must keep a copy of the chart on hand for use in enciphering and deciphering. Each plaintext letter is represented by a different combination of a's and b's. To write the word NOW, you would use abbaa for N, abbab for O and babaa for W:

abbaa   abbab   babaa
N   O   W

Try writing your name in the Baconian cipher on your worksheet.

Then solve the next two ciphers using the chart.

Cipher 55

baaba	baaaa	abbab	abbab	abbba	baaab
babaa	abaaa	ababa	ababa	ababb	aaaaa
abaab	aabaa	baaab	baabb	baaaa	abbba
baaaa	abaaa	baaab	aabaa	aaaaa	baaba
baaba	aaaaa	aaaba	abaab	aaaaa	baaba
aaabb	aaaaa	babaa	abbaa		

Cipher 56

aaaba	abbab	baabb	baaaa	aaaaa	aabba
aabaa	abaaa	baaab	aabab	aabaa	aaaaa
baaaa	baaba	aabbb	aaaaa	baaba	aabbb
aaaaa	baaab	baaab	aaaaa	abaaa	aaabb
abaaa	baaba	baaab	abbba	baaaa	aaaaa
babba	aabaa	baaaa	baaab		

Cipher 57

This time, instead of using a's and b's to write the cipher, let's use the numbers 4 and 8. Use 4 instead of a and 8 instead of b. Write out a new chart on your worksheet, using 4's and 8's. Start with A = 44444, B = 44448 and so on. Then solve the following:

84484	44888	44844	48884	48484	44444	48844
44844	84484	48444	84488	48884	48444	84484
44844	84444	48444	84448	48488	84488	44484
44888	44448	48444	44884	44884	44844	84444
84484	44888	44444	48844	44844	44444	84444
84484	44888					

Bacon's cipher can be used in many ingenious ways. If you have access to a typewriter, you could make up a chart using the asterisk (*) for a's and the dollar sign ($) for b's—or any other pair of symbols you like.

How about colored dots made with red and blue markers—red for a's and blue for b's?

All you need to create a Baconian cipher is two different letters, numbers or symbols. For very short messages, you might list girls' and boys' first names—girls' for a's and boys' for b's. This of course makes your cipher message even longer, so it wouldn't work well for long messages. The letter N which becomes Baconian abbaa (five times as long as N) would then become (in list form) Jane, Ted, Mike, Mary, Sue—18 letters to substitute for one!

On your worksheet, write down your own ideas for making up a Baconian cipher, and try out some cipher messages of your own.

● The Checkerboard Cipher

Why this cipher is called the checkerboard is not known. Perhaps it does look somewhat like a checkerboard, although there are not enough squares for it really to resemble one.

	1	2	3	4	5
1	A	K	L	U	V
2	B	I	M	T	W
3	C	H	N	S	X
4	D	G	O	R	Y
5	E	F	P	Q	Z

The numbers at the side and top of this alphabet square are used as substitutes for letters inside the square. Always select the side number (row) first and the top number (column) last. The letter A is represented by the number 11—first row, first column. The letter P is 53—fifth row, third column. The easiest way to "read" the substitute numbers is to note visually where row and column intersect.

Thus 11 = A, 12 = K, 13 = L and so on.

Write the solution to the following checkerboards on your worksheet, using the alphabet square shown for solving.

Cipher 58

11   53 45 44 11 23 22 41   22 34

53 44 43 43 52   24 32 11 24

24 32 51 44 51   22 34 33 24

11 13 25 11 45 34   44 43 43 23   11 24

24 32 51   24 43 53

Cipher 59

24 32 51 44 51   22 34   33 43

53 13 11 31 51   13 22 12 51   32 43 23 51

Notice that in the checkerboard square the letters of the alphabet were written first downward by column, then upward by column, then down again and so on. There are many different ways to write the alphabet in the square.

On your worksheet, rule off a 5 × 5 square and write the alphabet in it in a spiral route, starting at top left. The bottom row of your spiral should read NMLKI. (Notice that there is no room for J; it may be combined with I if necessary.)

Using the square you constructed, work out the next two problems.

Cipher 60

11   24 22 34 15   25 22 55 15 51 14

43 11 53 54 23   55 51   43 45 15 51

24 45 15   22 15 23 24   41 25   24 45 15

43 41 22 53 14   43 11 53 54 23   41 34 24

Cipher 61

31 15 41 31 53 15   43 45 41   45 11 44 15

31 15 22 23 41 51 11 53 55 24 32

31 53 34 23   11 22 15

23 41 52 15 24 55 52 15 23   52 55 51 34 23

15 44 15 22 32 24 45 55 51 35   15 53 23 15

● *More Checkerboards*

A keyword alphabet may of course be used in the square. The advantage of a keyword is that it is easier to remember a word followed by the rest of the alphabet than it is to remember a specific path the alphabet took in the square.

Here is an alphabet square constructed with the keyword ZEBRA.

	1	2	3	4	5
1	Z	E	B	R	A
2	C	D	F	G	H
3	I	K	L	M	N
4	O	P	Q	S	T
5	U	V	W	X	Y

Solve the next two ciphers using this alphabet square.

Cipher 62

31 23   55 41 51   22 41   35 41 45

21 33 31 34 13   45 41 41   25 31 24 25

55 41 51   53 31 33 33   35 41 45

23 15 33 33   45 41 41   23 15 14

Cipher 63

45 25 12   12 15 44 31 12 44 45   53 15 55

45 41   34 15 32 12   15   23 31 14 12

53 31 45 25   45 53 41   44 45 31 21 32 44

31 44   45 41   34 15 32 12   44 51 14 12

41 35 12   41 23   45 25 12 34   31 44

15   34 15 45 21 25

On your worksheet, using the square above, construct some short cipher sentences. Then try solving your own constructions—not only will you find errors if any occur,

but this exercise will help you learn how this cipher works.

Ready for a challenge? See if you can decipher the following without knowing exactly how the alphabet square was filled. A keyword was used, as in ciphers 62 and 63.

	1	2	3	4	5
1					
2				A	B
3	C	D	F	G	H
4	K	L	M	P	R
5	V	W	X	Y	Z

First use the letters already in the square to partially solve the cipher. Then list the missing letters, starting with E. Try to put those letters together to form an eight-letter keyword. Guessing at words in the cipher will help.

Cipher 64

14 22 43 13 15 21 43 13 14   24

31 22 52 24 45 32   25 13 31 22 43 13 14

24   35 13 45 22   25 13 31 24 12 14 13

35 13   45 24 23   15 35 13

52 45 22 23 34   52 24 54

What is the eight-letter keyword?

On your worksheet draw up several alphabet squares. Use keywords. Choose varying paths for the keyword and alphabet. Here are some long words you can use as keywords. They contain no repeated letters:

BLACKSMITH, MANUSCRIPT, PROFITABLE,

LUMBERJACK, TUMBLEDOWN, PERSONALITY,

COUNTRYSIDE, DISTURBANCE, SUBTROPICAL.

Make up a few short ciphers from your squares.

● *Codes*

What is the difference between a code and a cipher? Mainly that a code usually requires some kind of codebook. Also, in a code one word may stand for many words, although this is not always so. It is common practice to use the words cipher, code and cryptogram interchangeably. In fact, most of the "codes" in this and the next chapter are scarcely distinguishable from ciphers.

Look at the following sentence:

THE QUICK BROWN FOX JUMPS OVER THE LAZY DOG
 1   2   3   4   5   6   7   8   9

This sentence contains every letter of the alphabet. You might view the sentence as a wee codebook.

To compose a code from this "book," we use two numbers, the number assigned to the word (2 for QUICK, 6 for OVER) and the numbered position of the letter within the word that you want to use.

Suppose you want an E. There are E's in words 1, 6 and 7, and you may use any of these words. E would be first word, third letter (13) or sixth word, third letter (63) or seventh word, third letter (73).

More examples: N = 35   R = 32 or 64
D = 91

You and your cipher-solving friend would keep a copy of this sentence on hand.

Using the sentence, decipher this code:

Cipher 65

31 22 11 11 73 32 24 22 54 55   82 32 73

54 32 13 11 11 84   31 52 11   11 72 13 84

82 64 13   54 42 23 55 42 35 92 22 55

Note: For better secrecy, when constructing codes using the "brown fox" sentence, vary the cipher substitutes— use 33, 42, 61, 92 for O's, for example.

Cipher 66

23 24 13 24 32   63 82 53 23 55

82 31 92 22 11   42 35 73 72 82

81 41 82 23 32   31 22 71 55 11

23 81 81 11 82   55 71 13 55 93   42 92 91

An ordinary dictionary makes a fine codebook. You and your friend must have identical dictionaries, published in the same year. To use the dictionary for composing codes, you can use a page number to stand for a letter.

Suppose your message begins with the word MEET. Find any dictionary page that contains words beginning with M (and only M words, not a page that finishes M and starts N). If the M words run from page 714 to page 784, then any number between those two can stand for M. Your friend will open his identical dictionary, look up that page and see that all the words begin with M, so that is the first letter of your message.

Using *Webster's Ninth New Collegiate Dictionary* to encode the word MEET, you would find the M pages, pick a number, then the E pages, pick a number and so on.

M	E	E	T
774	392	434	1218

Of course other numbers may be used.

Use your worksheet and whatever dictionary you have to make up several short code messages using the method illustrated above.

Another method of using the dictionary for a coded message:

Find in the dictionary the first word of your message. PLAN appears on page 898 in Webster's Ninth, second column, 25th word in that column. Your cipher would then be 898–2–25.

You need not buy a big dictionary like Webster's Ninth. A small paperback dictionary will do just fine—but remember yours and your friend's must be identical.

You may also use a textbook or novel or any other book as a codebook.

Using a dictionary, write out on your worksheet some code sentences using the method above. You can see that using whole words instead of letters saves time, but the encoding takes more time.

A different kind of code is one you have already heard of—Morse code.

When written, Morse code consists of dots and dashes, but that would be a dead giveaway that it was Morse. Instead, let's use the number 1 for dots and the number 2 for dashes, a zero (0) for divisions between Morse letters and two 0's for divisions between Morse words. The letter A, in Morse, would be written 12. The word YOU would become 21220222011200.

A = 12	N = 21	
B = 2111	O = 222	
C = 2121	P = 1221	Using the number
D = 211	Q = 2212	symbols at the left,
E = 1	R = 121	solve the next two
F = 1121	S = 111	ciphers.
G = 221	T = 2	
H = 1111	U = 112	
I = 11	V = 1112	
J = 1222	W = 122	
K = 212	X = 2112	
L = 1211	Y = 2122	
M = 22	Z = 2211	

Cipher 67

1110 12110 10 10 122100   110 11100

20 11110 100   21110 10 1110 200

2110 2220 21210 20 2220 12100

Cipher 68

This time, the numbers are divided into groups of five. Watch those 0's!

11210 22201 21002 01111 01002 11011 01110

10120 11101 00222 01121 00111 02011 20211

10211 10222 01210 21021 01011 10111 00201

11101 01210 10011 01110 02102 22002 12101

12012 10100

Codes are much used in business. A coupon in a magazine may tell you to write to "Dept. PG." There probably is no department PG. The advertiser used code letters to tell him which magazine the coupon appeared in. Each magazine will have different code letters. His next ads will appear in those magazines that brought him the most orders.

For another business code we can look at any canned goods in the kitchen. On the can will appear the Universal Product Code—numbers and stripes in a little rectangle. The first five numbers on the symbol identify the maker— Green Giant, for example. The last five numbers tell what is inside the can—tender young sweet peas. The stripes duplicate that information. You can see that a code can indeed be a brief way to say a lot.

● *Cipher Fun*

Learning how to construct and solve ciphers is intriguing—but once you have learned how, what then?

To keep your skills sharp, you must use what you have learned. There are three practical ways to do this.

First, as suggested earlier, you might ask a friend to exchange cipher messages with you. Anyone can learn an easy cipher, such as the telephone cipher. For a more sophisticated type of cipher, your friend will have to be strongly oriented toward this hobby.

Second, you can subscribe to a magazine that offers ciphers to be solved. The puzzle magazines on newsstands are not the best for this. There are two excellent magazines you can subscribe to. For beginners, the better choice would be *Cryptography*, a 32-page bimonthly (published every other month) magazine containing about 125 ciphers. Among them are "specials"; send in the correct answers to these and earn points toward a "good solvers" certificate. This magazine offers plenty of solving clues for novices. For subscription information, write to: Cryptography, P.O. Box 641, Davis, CA 95617–0641. (Addresses and similar information given here are naturally subject to change.) Another magazine, *The Cryptogram*, contains some very difficult ciphers along with easier ones. *The Cryptogram* is published bimonthly by the American Cryptogram Association. For information on membership, which includes a subscription to the magazine, write to: ACA Treasurer, 12317 Dalewood Drive, Wheaton, MD 20902.

A third way to keep your ciphering skills in good order is to improve them by reading any of the many books currently available. Four titles on codes and ciphers published by Dover (available through your bookstore or directly from the publisher) are: Martin Gardner, *Codes, Ciphers and Secret Writing* (24761-9); Norma Gleason, *Cryptograms and Spygrams* (24036-3); Henry Lysing, *Secret Writing: An Introduction to Cryptograms, Ciphers and Codes* (23062-7); and Laurence Dwight Smith, *Cryptography: The Science of Secret Writing* (20247-X).

Using a Code Name

Spies and others who use codes and ciphers often use code names. A famous spy, Rudolf Roessler, a highly skilled agent for the Soviet espionage network, used the code name LUCY because he lived in Lucerne, Switzerland.

You too can adopt a code name. When exchanging cipher messages with a friend, sign your messages with the code name instead of your own.

Borrow the name of a celebrity. Why not? Engelbert Humperdinck did. The original Engelbert Humperdinck was a German composer who died in 1921, years before today's singer was born. The real name of the current Humperdinck (or at any rate the name his parents gave him) is Arnold Dorsey.

Or you could use a foreign-language version of your own first name: FRITZ instead of Fred (German); GIANNA instead of Jane (Italian); PEDRO, the Spanish equivalent of Peter; and so on.

Other ideas for a code name: names of cartoon characters, birds or animals or just any name that comes to mind, like SCARECROW from the television program *The Scarecrow and Mrs. King*.

Or switch around the letters of your name in some interesting way. A celebrated singer calls herself YMA SUMAC. What does that spell backwards?

In the world of cryptology, you can be anyone you want to be. Let your imagination soar.

Easy Transposition Ciphers

1. Bury treasure tonight.

2. Many happy returns.

3. Sending secret messages is fun.

4. If you want something you have to work for it.

5. Those who cannot bite should not show their teeth.

More Backward Ciphers

6. Liars need good memories.

7. Beware of black cats.

8. Meet me tonight at old mill.

9. Laughter is heard further than weeping.

10. A whitewashed crow soon shows black again.

The Null Cipher

11. This is a null cipher.

12. Send help.

13. Send help. (Same message.)

More Null Ciphers

14. Meet plane two p.m. tomorrow.

15. Have van at site tonight. Fast takeoff arranged.

Columnar Transpositions

16. Ghost stories.

More Columnar Transpositions

17. Stars are gigantic balls of superheated gases.

18. A smile is a curve that helps to set things straight.

19. The fool in a hurry drinks his tea with a fork.

20. Only ten people out of one thousand own a TV set in Zimbabwe.

21. Hummingbirds can fly backward.

22.

Step 1					*Step 2*			
1	2	3	4		4	2	3	1
D	O	N	O		O	O	N	D
T	A	S	K		K	A	S	T
T	H	E	W		W	H	E	T
A	Y	O	F		F	Y	O	A
A	B	L	I		I	B	L	A
N	D	M	A		A	D	M	N
N	X	X	X		X	X	X	N

Final cipher: OKWFI AXOAH YBDXN SEOLM XDTTA ANN

Route Transpositions

23.

1		2		3		4	
Y	S	H	A	Y	T	H	A
P	E	P	P	P	I	S	P
P	M	Y	T	P	M	E	P
A	I	M	I	A	E	M	Y
H	T	E	S	H	S	I	T

24. Half a loaf is better than none.

25. There is no elbow that bends outward.

26. The best way to keep milk from getting sour is to leave it in the cow. (Read the message in columns, first down, then up.)

Easy Substitution Ciphers

27. Dead men tell no tales.

28. One old friend is better than two new ones.

29. UIF TUBUVF PG MJCFSUZ

30. VJG RGCPWV KU C HTWKV PQV C PWV

31. D SUXQH LV D SOXP WKDW KDV VHHQ EHWWHU GDBV

More Substitution Ciphers

32. If ants are so busy, how come they have time to attend all the picnics?

33. The windshield wiper was invented so police would have a place to put parking tickets.

34. I eat my peas with honey/I've done it all my life/It makes the peas taste funny/But it keeps them on the knife.

35. A hospital is a place where people who are run down wind up. (Uses the E cipher alphabet.)

36. Table tennis is the unofficial sport of China. (C cipher alphabet.)

37. IBM. (International Business Machines, a company that makes sophisticated computers.)

More Easy Substitution Ciphers

38. The dachshund is a dog that is only half a dog high but a dog and a half long.

39. The most wasted of all days is the day when we have not laughed.

40. The alphabet would end with the last letters identical with those in the normal alphabet. If that doesn't bother you, go ahead and start the keyword at the beginning of the cipher alphabet.

41. If you have an itch to write, the best thing to use is a scratch pad.

42. Conscience is the voice that tells you not to do something after you have done it.

Random Substitution Ciphers

43. Captain Steele outwits Daddy Warbucks.

44. Little Willie, home from school,/Where he learned the Golden Rule,/Said, "If I eat up this cake/Sis won't have a stomach ache."

More About Random Substitutions

45. In the first auto race ever held, more than ninety years ago, the winner averaged a speed of seven and a half miles per hour.

46. The only state in this country where diamonds can be found is Arkansas. Tourists are allowed to dig for them.

47. The letter E is the beginning of eternity, the end of time and space, the beginning of every end, the end of every place.

Easy Telephone Ciphers

48. The crow is a bird that never complains without caws.

49. Letting the cat out of the bag is much easier to do than putting it back.

50. A computer is almost human except it never blames its mistakes on other computers.

More Telephone Ciphers

51. It is hard for an empty sack to stand upright.

52. All clear for raid tonight.

53. One person's stumbling block is another's stepping stone.

54. One cannot expect the watchdog to bite himself.

Sir Francis Bacon's Cipher

55. Troops will make surprise attack at dawn.

56. Courage is fear that has said its prayers.

57. The planet Jupiter is much bigger than Earth.

The Checkerboard Cipher

58. A pyramid is proof that there isn't always room at the top.

59. There is no place like home.

60. A true friend walks in when the rest of the world walks out.

61. People who have personality plus are sometimes minus everything else.

More Checkerboards

62. If you do not climb too high you will not fall too far.

63. The easiest way to make a fire with two sticks is to make sure one of them is a match.

64. Sometimes a coward becomes a hero because he ran the wrong way. (Keyword = QUESTION.)

Codes

65. Buttercups are pretty but they are poisonous.

66. Ice cream is about one-half air but still tastes good.

More Codes

67. Sleep is the best doctor.

68. For the disease of stubbornness there is no cure.